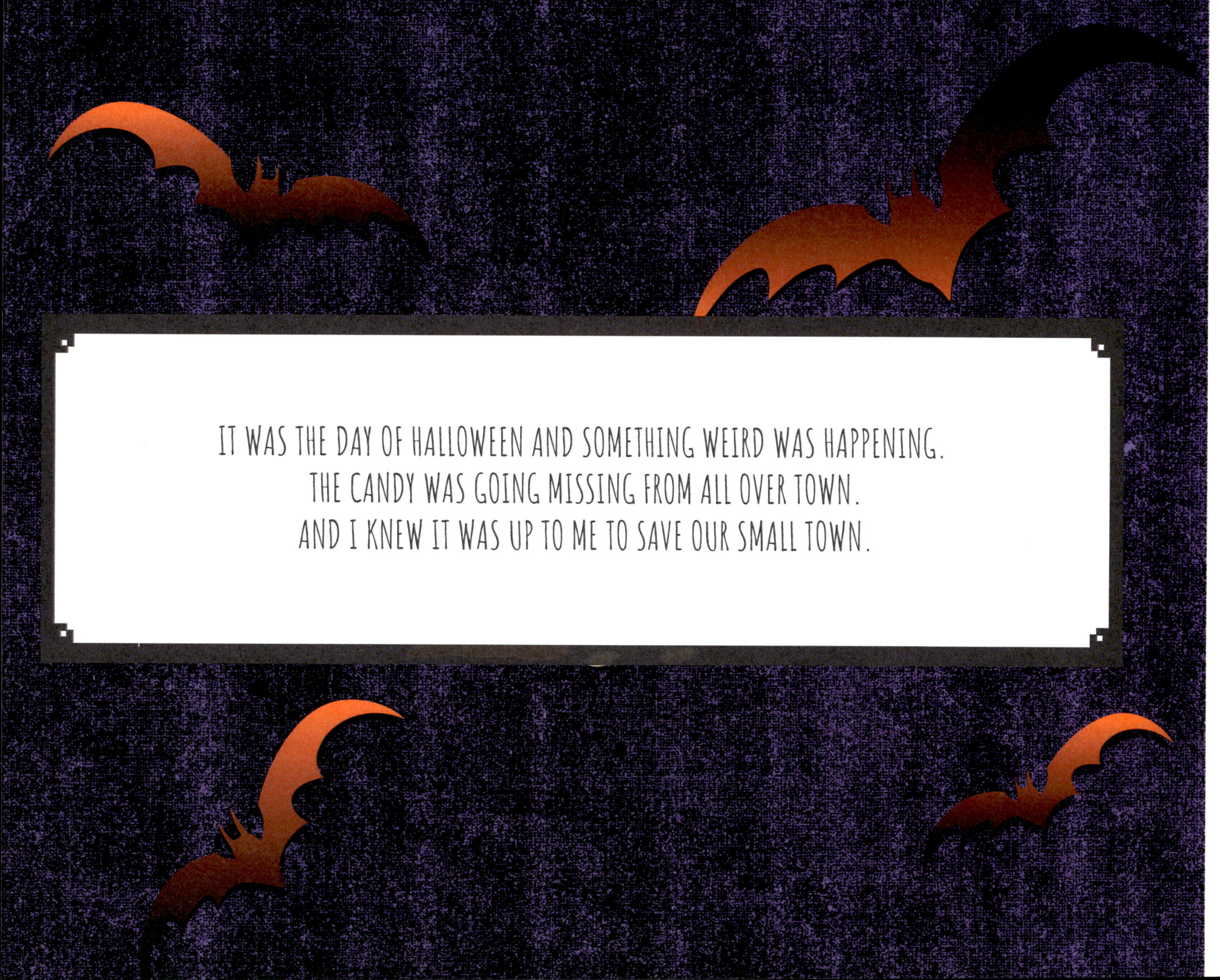

IT WAS THE DAY OF HALLOWEEN AND SOMETHING WEIRD WAS HAPPENING.
THE CANDY WAS GOING MISSING FROM ALL OVER TOWN.
AND I KNEW IT WAS UP TO ME TO SAVE OUR SMALL TOWN.

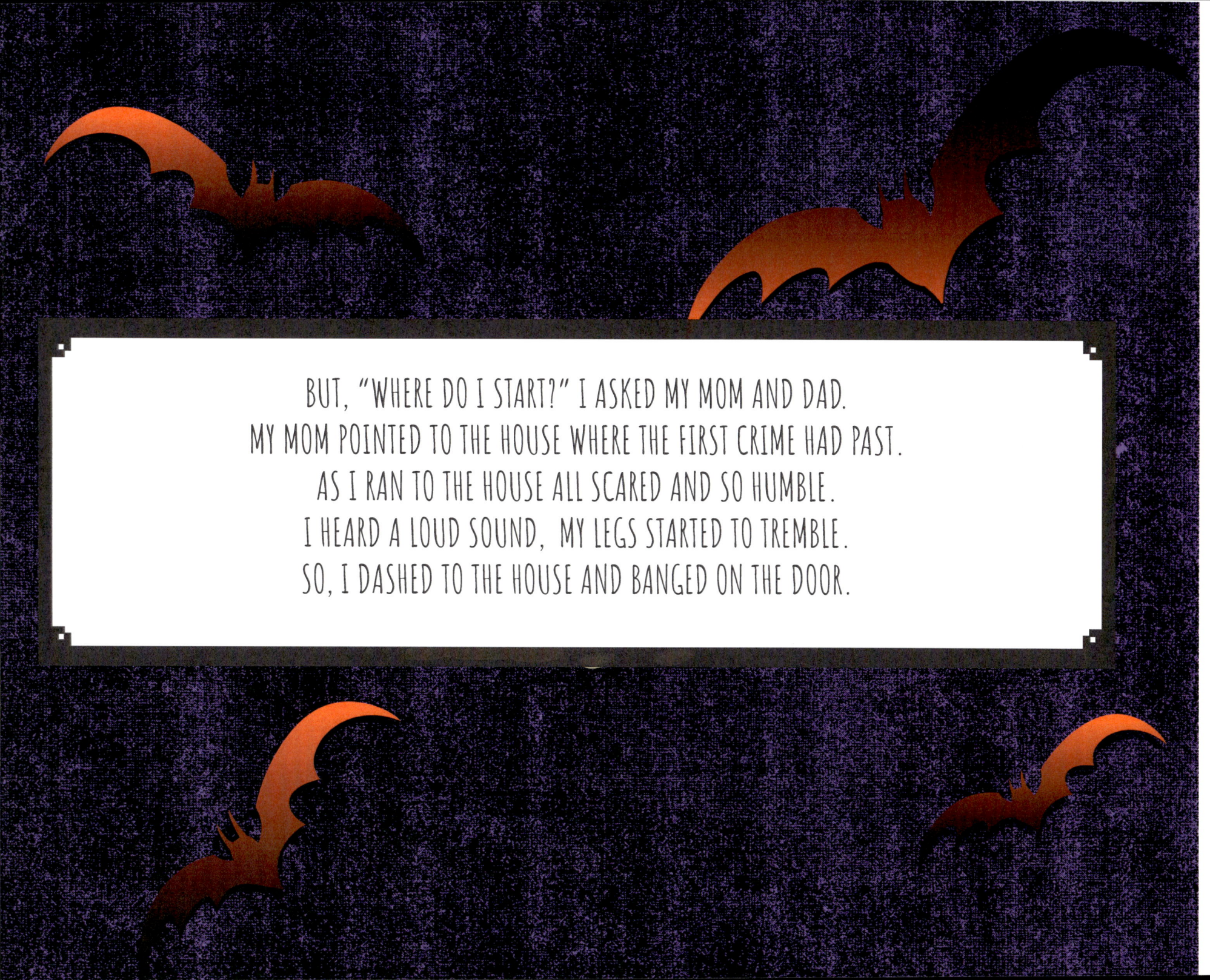

BUT, "WHERE DO I START?" I ASKED MY MOM AND DAD.
MY MOM POINTED TO THE HOUSE WHERE THE FIRST CRIME HAD PAST.
AS I RAN TO THE HOUSE ALL SCARED AND SO HUMBLE.
I HEARD A LOUD SOUND, MY LEGS STARTED TO TREMBLE.
SO, I DASHED TO THE HOUSE AND BANGED ON THE DOOR.

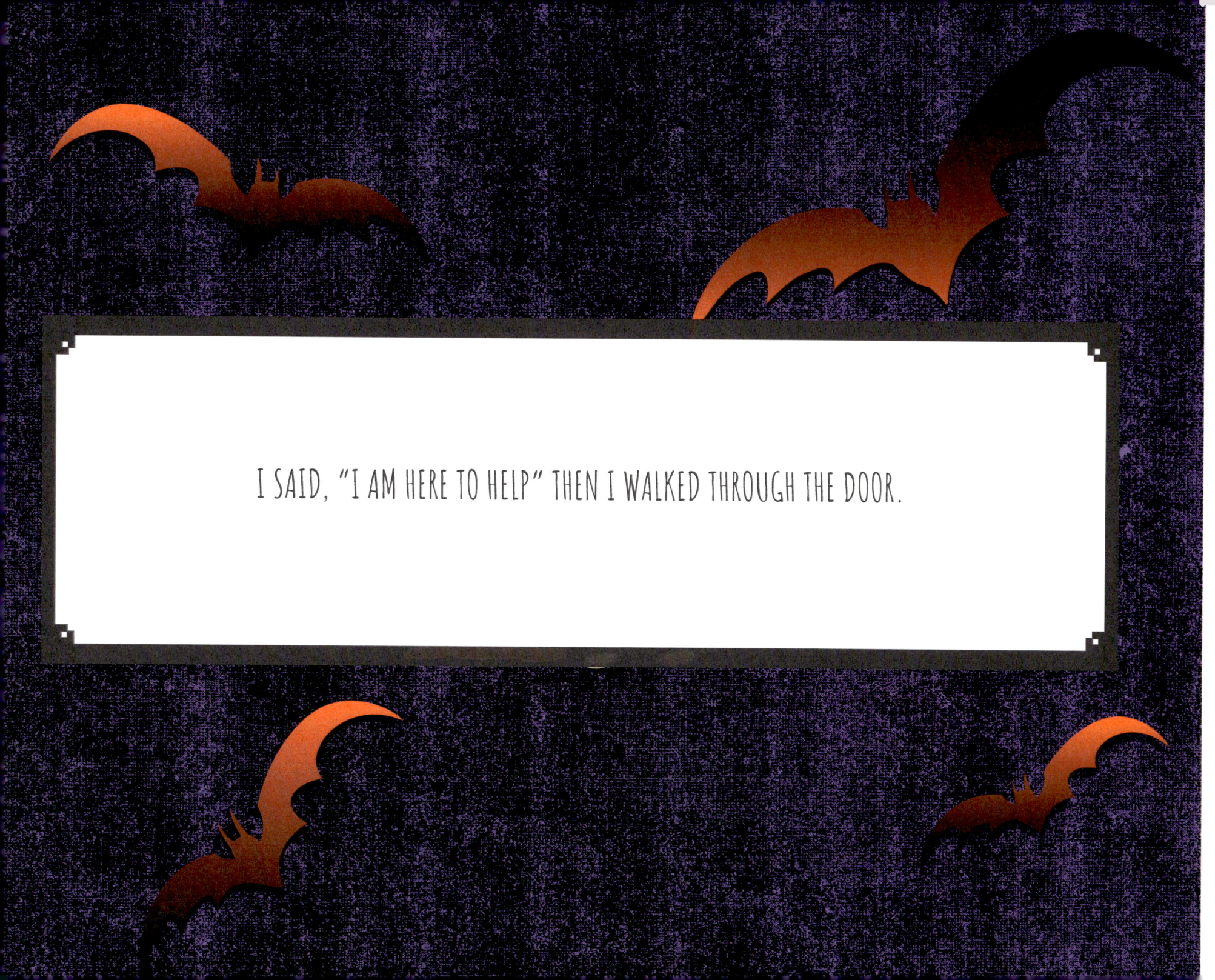

I SAID, "I AM HERE TO HELP" THEN I WALKED THROUGH THE DOOR.

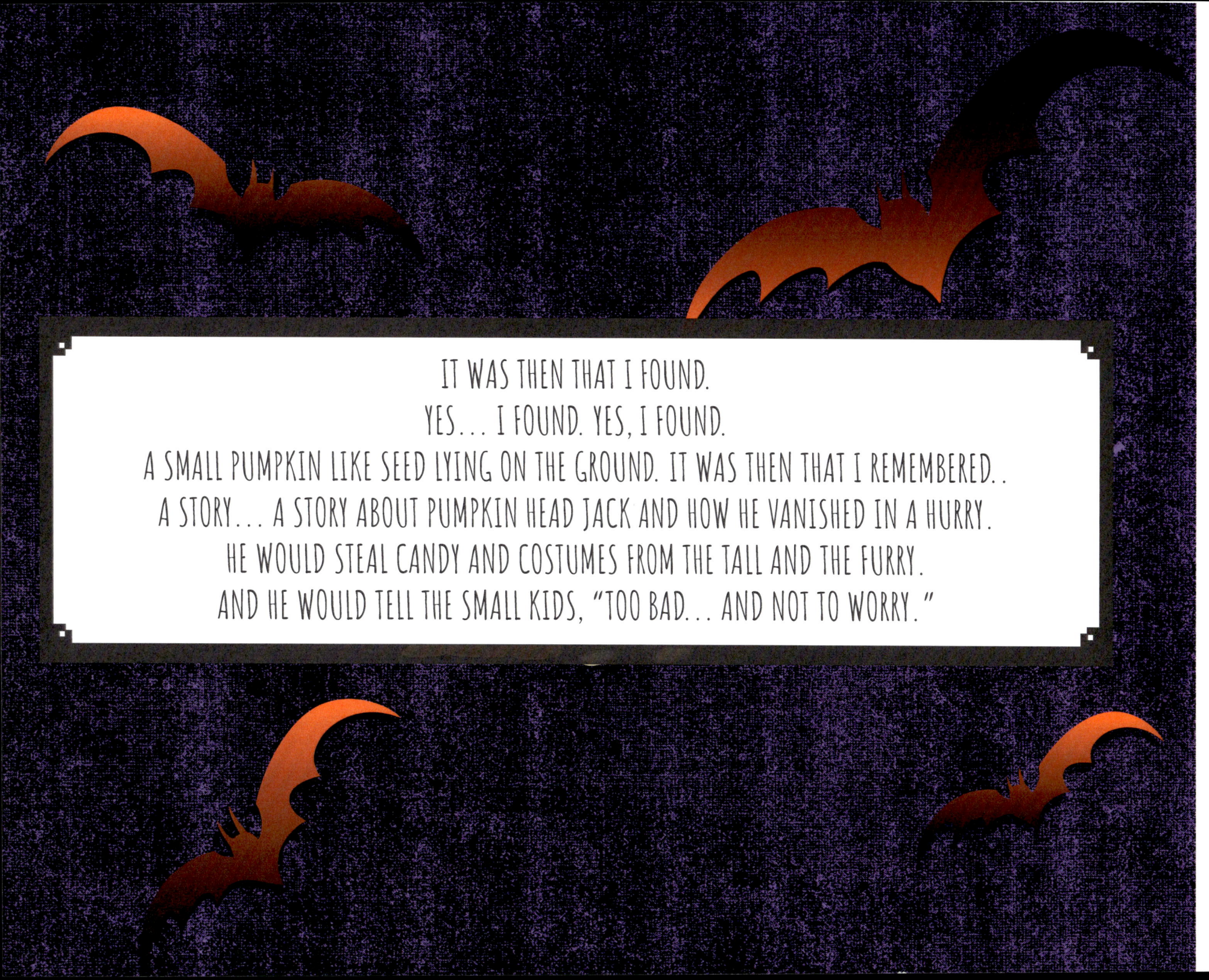

IT WAS THEN THAT I FOUND.
YES… I FOUND. YES, I FOUND.
A SMALL PUMPKIN LIKE SEED LYING ON THE GROUND. IT WAS THEN THAT I REMEMBERED..
A STORY… A STORY ABOUT PUMPKIN HEAD JACK AND HOW HE VANISHED IN A HURRY.
HE WOULD STEAL CANDY AND COSTUMES FROM THE TALL AND THE FURRY.
AND HE WOULD TELL THE SMALL KIDS, "TOO BAD… AND NOT TO WORRY."

AS I GATHER THE CLUES, I HEARD A LOUD SCREAM.
IT WAS COMING FROM THE HOUSE RIGHT NEXT TO MY FRIEND STEVE.
I DASHED TO THE WINDOW AND YOU WOULD NOT BELIEVE.
IT WAS PUMPKIN HEAD JACK LURKING BEHIND A TREE.

I GOT CLOSER AND CLOSER TO PUMPKIN HEAD JACK.
IT WAS THEN THAT I HEARD HIS NEXT PLAN OF ATTACK.
I HID AND I WAITED WHILE HE TURNED HIS BACK.
THEN HE DASHED INTO TOWN TO STEAL ALL THE TOWN'S SNACKS.

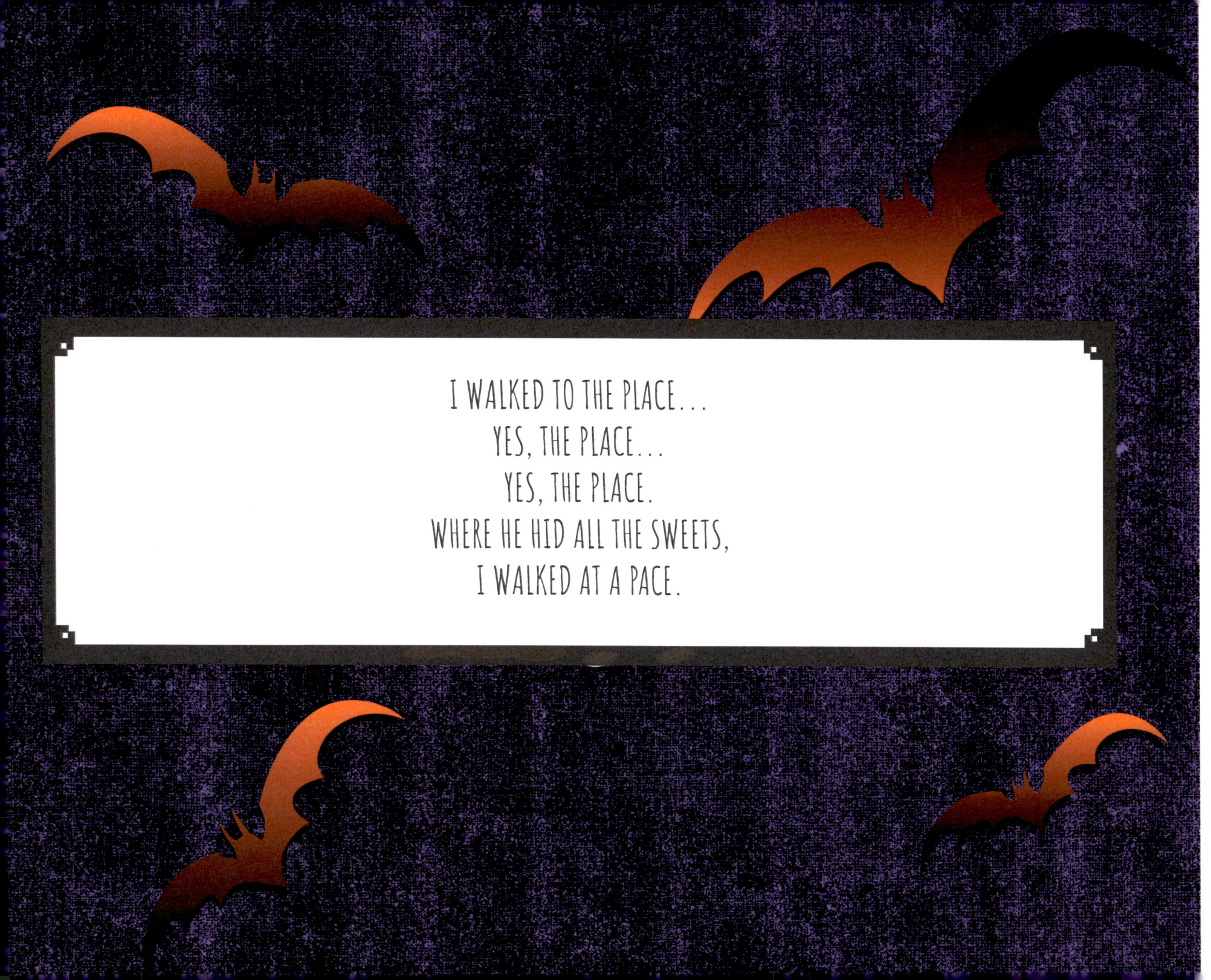

I WALKED TO THE PLACE…
YES, THE PLACE…
YES, THE PLACE.
WHERE HE HID ALL THE SWEETS,
I WALKED AT A PACE.

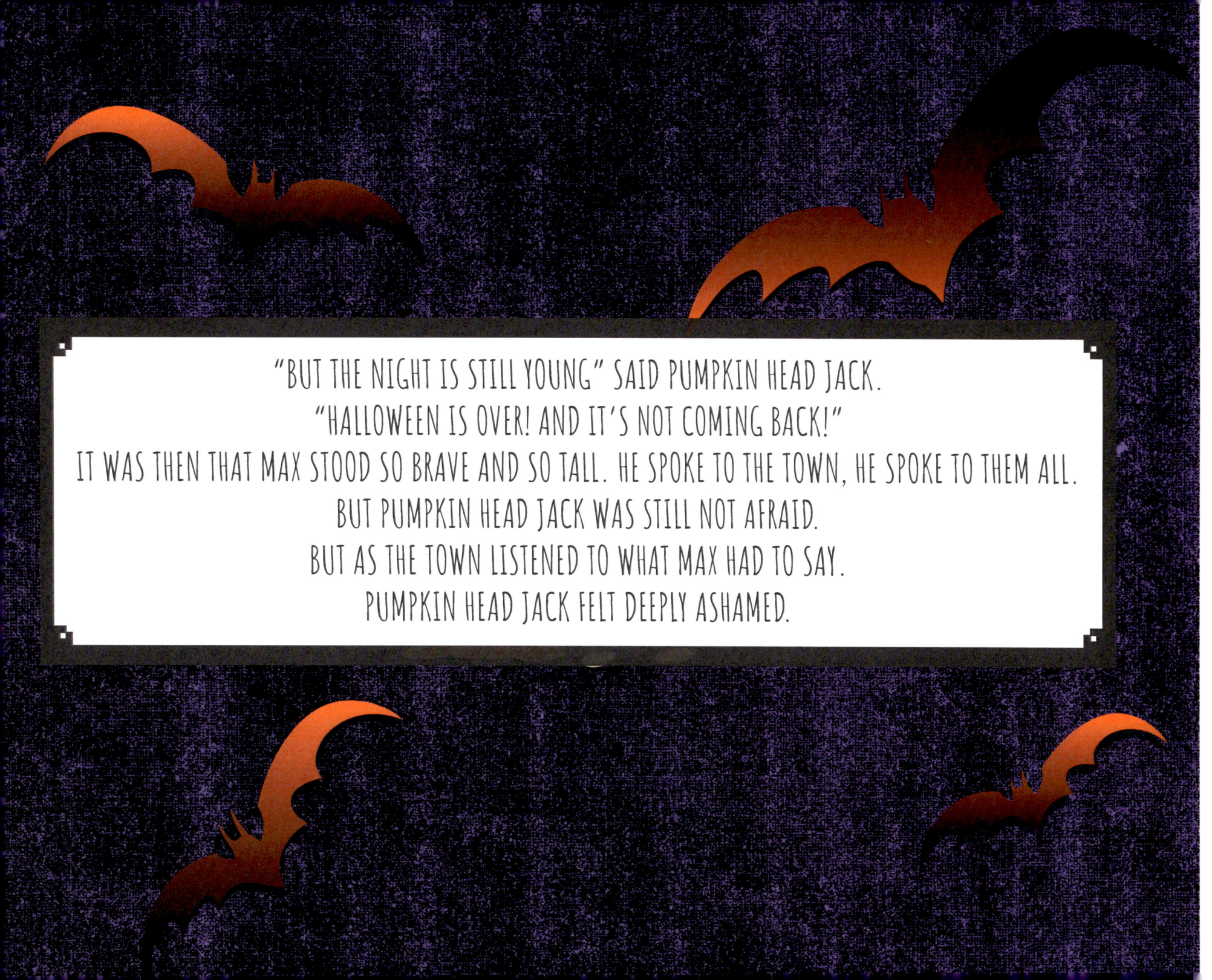

"BUT THE NIGHT IS STILL YOUNG" SAID PUMPKIN HEAD JACK.
"HALLOWEEN IS OVER! AND IT'S NOT COMING BACK!"
IT WAS THEN THAT MAX STOOD SO BRAVE AND SO TALL. HE SPOKE TO THE TOWN, HE SPOKE TO THEM ALL.
BUT PUMPKIN HEAD JACK WAS STILL NOT AFRAID.
BUT AS THE TOWN LISTENED TO WHAT MAX HAD TO SAY.
PUMPKIN HEAD JACK FELT DEEPLY ASHAMED.

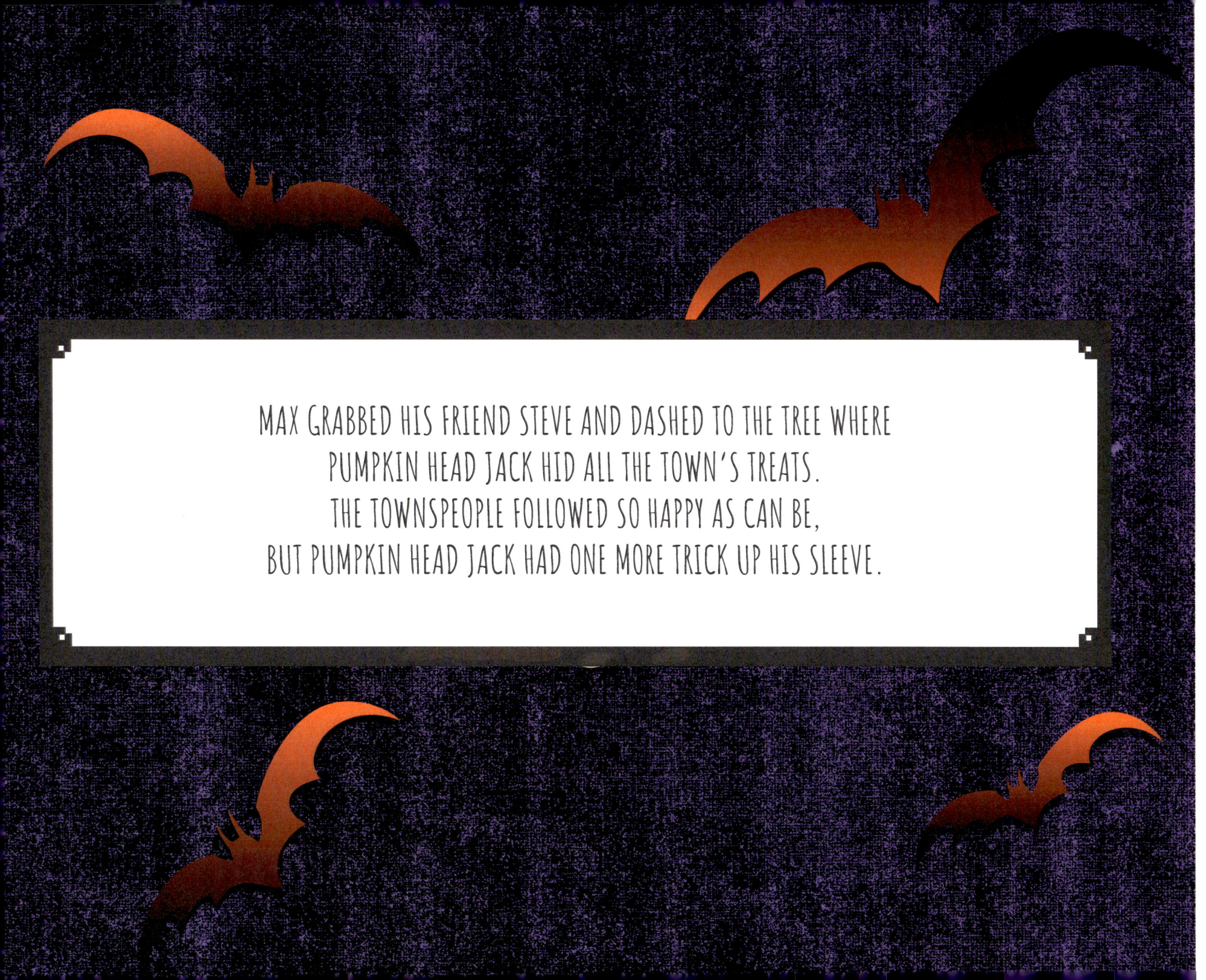

MAX GRABBED HIS FRIEND STEVE AND DASHED TO THE TREE WHERE
PUMPKIN HEAD JACK HID ALL THE TOWN'S TREATS.
THE TOWNSPEOPLE FOLLOWED SO HAPPY AS CAN BE,
BUT PUMPKIN HEAD JACK HAD ONE MORE TRICK UP HIS SLEEVE.

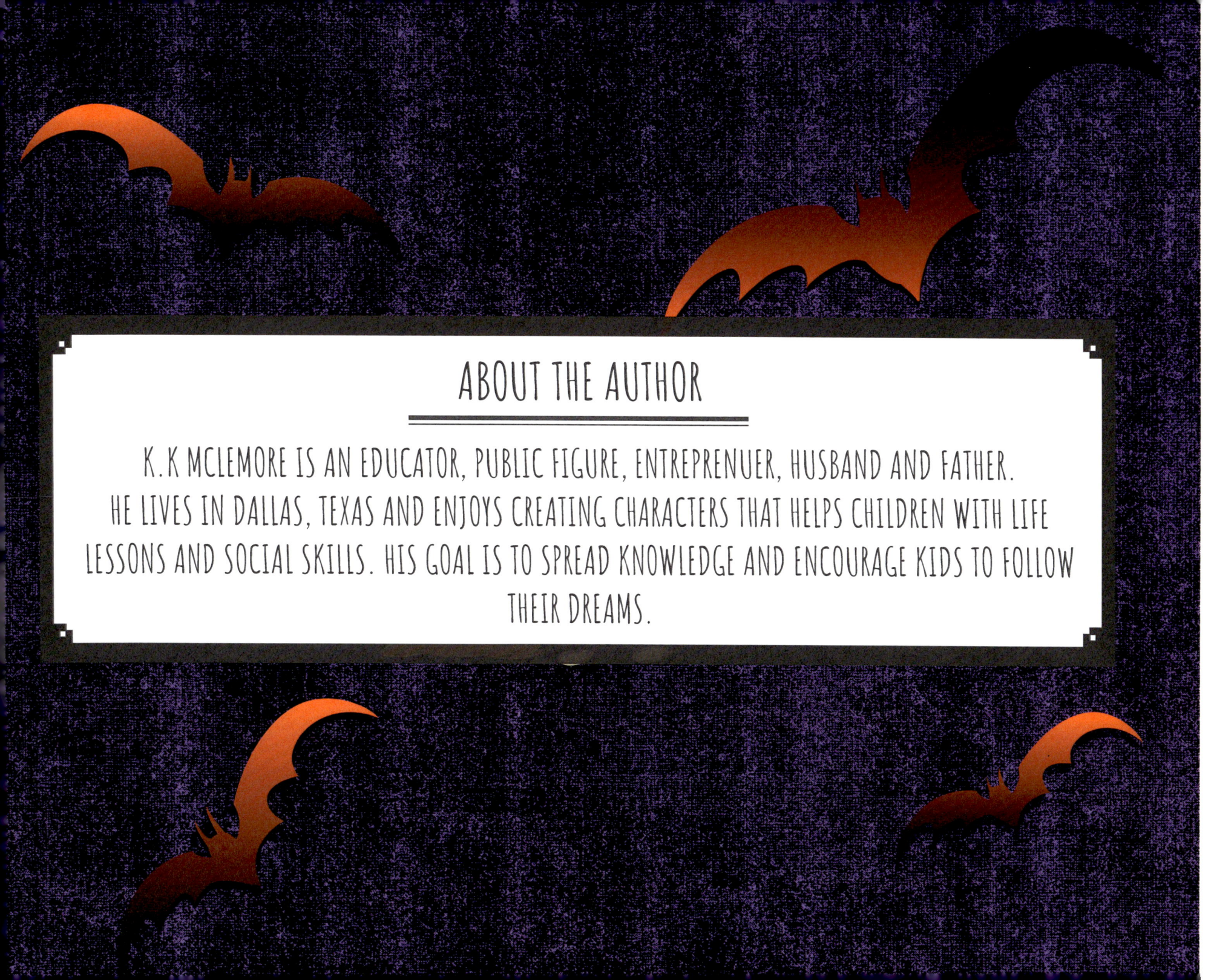

ABOUT THE AUTHOR

K.K MCLEMORE IS AN EDUCATOR, PUBLIC FIGURE, ENTREPRENUER, HUSBAND AND FATHER. HE LIVES IN DALLAS, TEXAS AND ENJOYS CREATING CHARACTERS THAT HELPS CHILDREN WITH LIFE LESSONS AND SOCIAL SKILLS. HIS GOAL IS TO SPREAD KNOWLEDGE AND ENCOURAGE KIDS TO FOLLOW THEIR DREAMS.

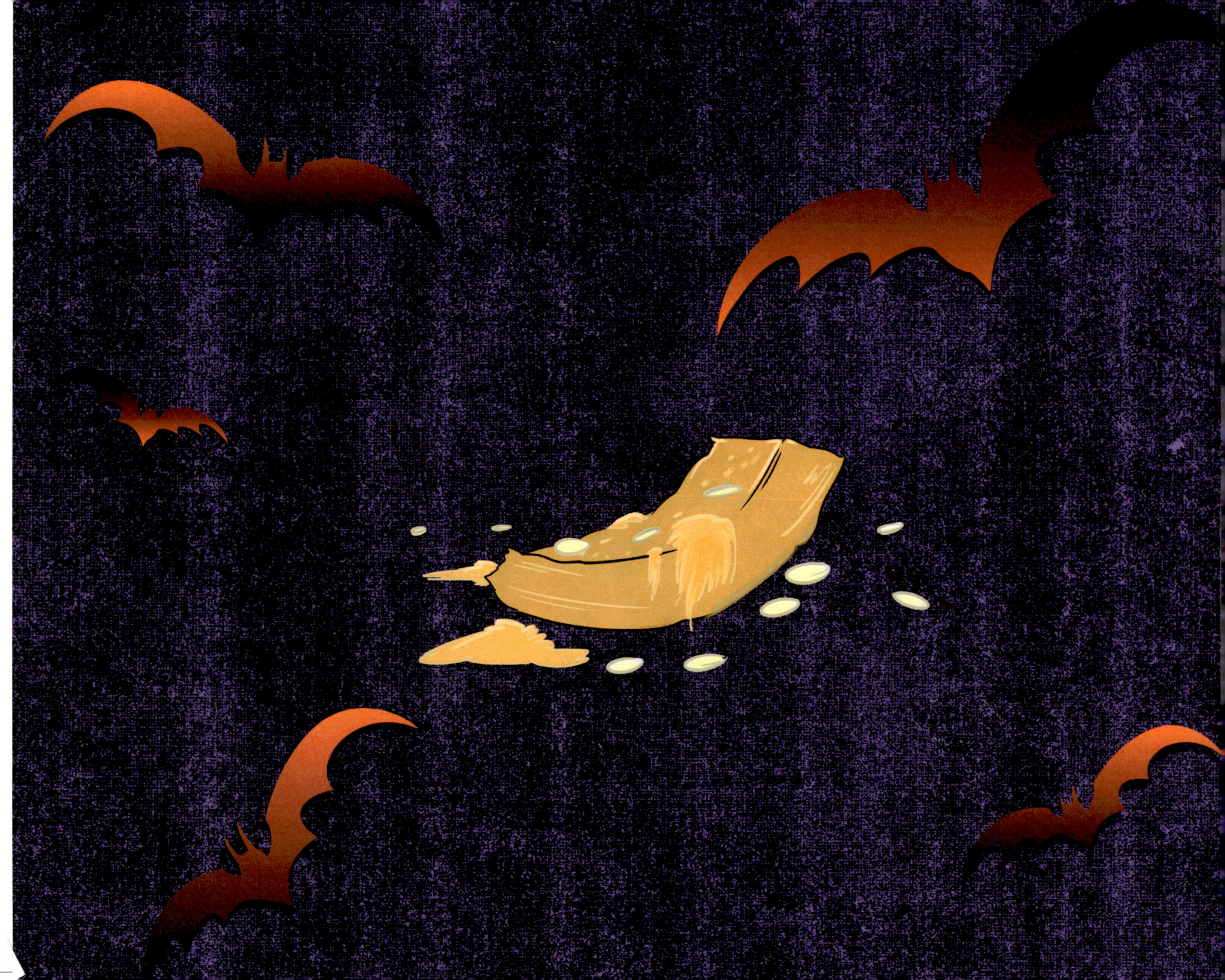

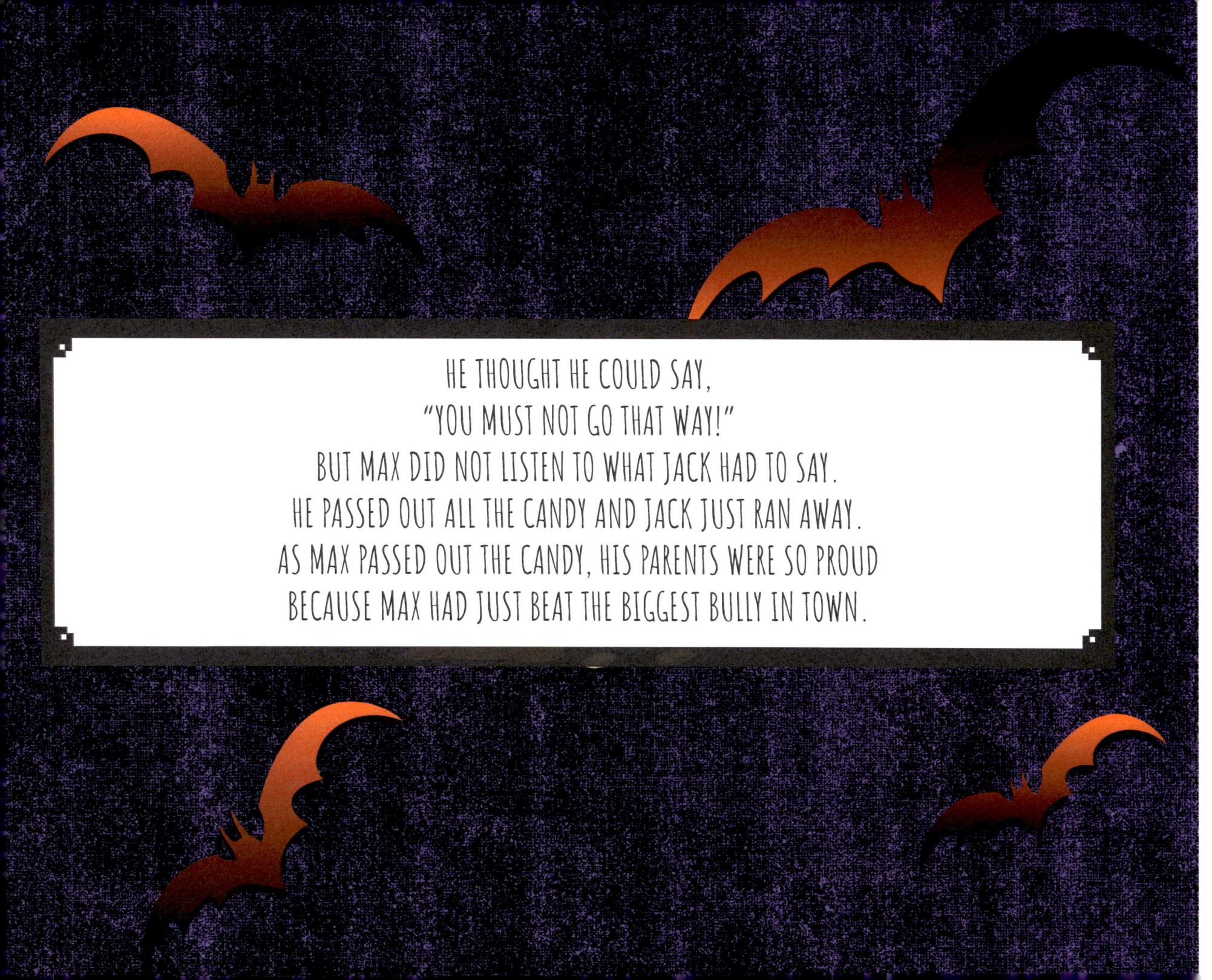

HE THOUGHT HE COULD SAY,
"YOU MUST NOT GO THAT WAY!"
BUT MAX DID NOT LISTEN TO WHAT JACK HAD TO SAY.
HE PASSED OUT ALL THE CANDY AND JACK JUST RAN AWAY.
AS MAX PASSED OUT THE CANDY, HIS PARENTS WERE SO PROUD
BECAUSE MAX HAD JUST BEAT THE BIGGEST BULLY IN TOWN.